THE EUCHARIST
Mystery of Friendship

The CHRISTIAN IDENTITY SERIES allows the modern layman to find meaning in the teachings of Christ, to help him anchor his personality in ageless values, to show him how christianity can be lived today. The series provides the layman with information about the human condition, the questions life raises, and the solutions that the gospel message can offer to existence. Since christian identity cannot be found in isolation, the series addresses itself to the total human community. It is designed for private reading, for classes in religious education, and for study groups. Each volume contains discussion questions, suggestions for further readings, and multi-media.

MATTHEW EUSSEN, EDITOR
Center for Studies in Religious Education

THE
EUCHARIST

MYSTERY OF FRIENDSHIP

BY *Bernard Cooke* S.J.

EDITED BY MATTHEW EUSSEN
FROM A SERIES OF LECTURES

Christian Identity Series

Geo. A. Pflaum, Publisher

DAYTON • OHIO • 1969

Imprimi potest: Very Rev. Joseph D. Sheehan, S.J.

Nihil obstat: Cletus Wessels, S.T.D., Censor Deputatus

Imprimatur: ✛ James J. Byrne, S.T.D.
Archbishop of Dubuque
August 20, 1969

BX
2215.2
.C6

4

Photo Credits: Alan Oddie: pages 51, 55; Paul Tucker: pages 8, 15, 21, 28, 35, 46, 61, 68, 84, 91, 96, 101, 106, 124.

Library of Congress Catalogue Card Number: 70-97040

Copyright © 1969 by Bernard Cooke, S.J.

GEO. A. PFLAUM, PUBLISHER
38 West Fifth Street, Dayton, Ohio 45402

Manufactured in the United States of America

Contents

THE EUCHARIST
Mystery of Friendship

Board.

One for "All"
ALL for "One"
D. O.
Dayton Originations

ONE

The Community of Man and the Eucharist

WHILE A COLD technological world seems to force isolation and anonymity, contemporary man must search for meaning. While conveyor belts and computers take over human productivity, modern man is challenged to survive as a person. Human dignity and freedom have a precarious future in a mechanized world, unless man is capable of asserting his creative ability in the community of man. As the products of our own culture continue to massage us into passivity, each one of us can lose his position as creator and master of his own destiny.

A sense of mastery and belonging is rapidly disappearing as ethnic groups undergo a diaspora. The sense of belonging to one's own people, to one's own group, to one's own culture is not ours. The metropolis is not a collection of small national ghettoes, but a center of technology which collects men and

women as a task force. The self-sufficient
community with its own traditions is disappearing. Each man stands alone. Each man
can no longer rely on codes and customs that
his parents and their parents had declared
sacred. He must find his identity elsewhere.
Contemporary man must search for values
that will offer meaning and significance to his
existence.

Even though the loss of a sense of belonging and identity is very real, our culture has
produced signs of hope for a world community, a community of mankind in which each
person can find meaning. Technology, which
can be so cold and ruthless, offers bonds of
union and communication that unite men
from all corners of the world.

One of the salient features of the modern
world is the growing interdependence of men
one on the other, a development promoted
chiefly by modern technical advances. Never-
theless brotherly dialogue among men does not
reach its perfection on the level of technical
progress, but on the deeper level of interpersonal relationships. These demand a mutual
respect for the full spiritual dignity of the person. (*Pastoral Constitution on the Church in
the Modern World*, n. 23)

Technology offers new hope. Advances in communication can make real the community for which man is searching. The filth of the slums, the misery of undeveloped nations, the starving faces of the poor are brought into the living rooms of elite suburban homes. Each newscast and each daily paper bring a cry for help from war-torn nations.

As small self-contained communities break up and are absorbed, we are bombarded with invitations to participate in the greater community of man, the world-community, the community of nations. These invitations to join the brotherhood of men are futile if we as christians do not join our efforts to our neighbor's.

It is ironic that the christian, who has a mandate from the Word of God to found the community of men, can ignore the various movements of history. God, in the promises of his salvation, has always stressed that salvation will be wrought only through the community of men. Men will not be saved without their fellow men. By various fates of history, the citizen, the state, the church and the world are forced to turn their attention to the most important idea in biblical literature, namely, community. Although modern culture offers the means whereby community can become a reality, each christian must make a response to those means.

> God, who has fatherly concern for everyone, has willed that all men should constitute one family and treat one another in a spirit of brotherhood. For having been created in the image of God, who "from one man has created the whole human race and made them live all over the face of the earth" (Acts 17:26), all men are called to one and the same goal, namely God himself.
>
> To men growing daily more dependent on one another, and to a world becoming more unified every day, this truth proves to be of paramount importance. (*Pastoral Constitution on the Church in the Modern World*, n. 24)

Even though community has perhaps lost much of its meaning in our times, it cannot be passed over lightly. If modern man is to survive, he must learn to communicate. This implies that he must develop a willingness to share and to make a response. Community means communing, a communion. The New Testament's first understanding of *koinonia*, church, is a community par excellence. As the early theologians developed the implications found in the New Testament, they emphasized that there must be sharing; there must be participation; there must be communication. While men living under the same roof may not have anything resembling a community, men separated geographically may be profoundly bound into a community.

The early christians had a profound sense of being part of the same reality. Within the immediate group they held all things in common. They shared their goods with those christians in dire straits. One need only to recall Paul's appeal to the Greek churches for the suffering church in Jerusalem. As the message of the gospel was being preached in the Mediterranean basin, pockets of christians developed. Even within the first fifty years the church was already called catholic, universal. The Roman empire could not for long consider these christians merely isolated groups. The christians themselves were aware of unity and the pagans were forced to accept this fact. What joined the first christians was a sense of being united in something they shared. What these christians shared was their love for one another expressed by their participation in the eucharist.

If modern man is to form a community out of his world, he must capture the sense of union that the early christian felt with his fellow man. Whether we are speaking of a small community, the church, or the world community, we must ask ourselves what is the basis for unity? What is meant to make us one?

To form a community there must be communication. The means of communication are already present in our culture, but the christian has not as yet realized their value and importance for himself and the rest of mankind. The communications media are our invitation to join the world. So frequently we criticize our leaders for not doing something about the grave problems that surround us. But this is a misunderstanding of our own obligation. Throughout history, the greatest breakdown of community occurred when authority had to assume total responsibility for unity.

History teaches us the lesson that the communication process will ground a genuine

community in the church which is not from the top down only. The Holy Spirit does not work just in those who are in authority. The Holy Spirit works in the entire church. Historically, we have lost immensely in the life of the church and its apostolic function because we have not trusted the Spirit at work in the world. Many times the church assumed that the world is something to be saved, that the world is to be instructed, that the world is to be talked to and not communicated with. At this time, the church cannot afford not to listen to the world. We christians must listen; we must give ear to the Spirit of God abroad in the world. As we become more aware that the world's mission is also that of the church, we must communicate with the world so that the best efforts in our culture will not be lost.

Since the church has a visible and social structure as a sign of her unity in Christ, she can and ought to be enriched by the development of human social life, not that there is any lack in the constitution given her by Christ, but that she can understand it more penetratingly, express it better, and adjust it more successfully to our times. (*Pastoral Constitution on the Church in the Modern World*, n. 44)

If the incarnation has any meaning it is that God united himself with our world and that he is at work in our history. The christian must therefore learn to listen to the actions of the Holy Spirit. Some of the finest inspirations for apostolic endeavors come from those which arise from the needs in the human community. Communication with the world is essential if the christian is to have a role in building a community of mankind according to the plan of God.

Real communication in both directions involves sharing of deep concern, of worries, of ideas, of dreams. All must be shared. Only when they are shared will there be unified personal endeavor. The christian must share himself with the world as the world shares itself with him. One of the most basic laws of human relationships is that if someone does not open himself to me, I will not be open to him. The emphasis in current theology is that the church is a family where members are concerned for one another. This emphasis in our theology has biblical roots and certainly can and should be extended to the family of man.

We as christians must learn to share our vision of faith. We have a vision of life; we have a common love and we approach the matter of loving people from an aspect which is unique to the christian family.

If the christian is not in dialogue with his culture, he is professing beliefs that have no meaning for his fellow man. To be active christians, to be a vital church, we need communication. We need to share what we possess with all men in order to build a unity of brotherhood, a community of mankind.

We might well ask ourselves what should be the function of really welding a genuine spirit of community. Although we have indicated that the development of the world seems to be a sweep toward unity, there is no inner ultimate meaning in this historical movement apart from Christ. In fact, within this very evolution toward unity there are elements that have power to destroy the very center of man. Therefore the christian cannot idly stand by and let history simply happen. He must bring meaning through the eucharist to this movement toward unity. This is the theological answer and one not readily understood.

The eucharist is the sacrament of unity and must be studied as an expression of unity. If it is to be the supreme symbol of a unity that can bring meaning to our culture, it must really be central to the life of the community, at least the christian community.

The eucharist is the crossroad of human history. Everything comes to focus here. The progression of the human race is a movement of each succeeding generation's participation in the eucharist. Everything we know about man, about the world, about God comes to focus there. In the eucharist all of history takes on meaning because it is united in the one person, Jesus Christ. In the eucharist the fullness of history is achieved, for in its symbolism there is presented all of the past, present and future. There is within it a unity that ties the first just man to the last of the redeemed. Within this sacrament there are found the inspirations and the aspirations to form the human community, because this sacrament gives value and meaning to human life. It gives to the movement of history a direction and a purpose, because it celebrates the mystery of the presence of Christ.

What the christian brings to his culture and to history is the mystery of Christ's presence. Without a realization of this presence and its uniqueness in the eucharist, the christian has little to offer his times. If Christ's presence is not real to him and participation in the eucharist a mere formality, he has little of value to give to his fellow man.

The very heart of the church as a community is precisely that she is the community of Christ. The church is the sacrament of Christ, the body of Christ, because she is the visible expression of the risen Christ. If this presence is not real to the members of the christian community, the church has no claim to be the zenith of the human community, because Christ does not live in her as the risen Lord. Without the reality of Christ's presence christianity would be reduced to faith in a message left by a great founder. And the christian community would share no more than a common belief in dead doctrines.

The presence of Christ today is the finality of Christ's risen humanity. The New Testament bears adequate witness to the fact that Christ rose for our sakes. Without his pres-

ence to men, Christ would not be in risen life. Christ chose his new glorified life to give himself more fully to his brothers and sisters. This choice to give himself to men continues to dominate the consciousness of Christ even as risen Lord. The eucharist is the symbol and the reality of this self-giving.

However, before we can understand the reality of Christ's presence in the eucharist, we must first look at our faith experience. We do not have a direct experience of Christ's presence among us. Our faith experience certainly is not that we hear, see or touch Christ. We do not experience the ordinary ways in which one person is present to another. The normal indications of an interpersonal relationship are not found in our relationship with Christ. Therefore we seem to be forced to conclude that Christ is removed from us and not really present in any human way.

Such a conclusion is too facile. It is true that our normal relationships with others involve geographical proximity. Even when we become present to another person at a distance, there is a spatial link, a letter or the human voice over the telephone. However, the reality of presence need not involve such spatial presence. Presence between persons is essentially a matter of communication. The process whereby one person becomes conscious of another person is the reality of presence. It is the process whereby one person becomes interior to another. True personal presence is not a question of spatial proximity; rather it is a question of awareness. Presence is the reality of two people entering into conscious communion with one another.

There are limitless levels of identification in the reality of personal communication. At a bus stop I may say "good evening" to a stranger. In that case I extend my communication in a very limited way. A conversation with a friendly neighborhood grocer would create a deeper awareness of another. When I am sharing my confidences with a very close friend, my presence to him and his presence to me are uniquely different. I would be revealing myself as a person to this friend. I would be giving myself in my deepest consciousness of myself. During this conversation, at least, I would be existing for this other person. In true friendship this being for another person would endure as a constitutive factor in my own personal identity. To be for my friend would be part of what it means for me to be me.

The critical element in presence is to be, to exist, for another person. Although for us space and time are linked to presence, spatial nearness is accidental to the basic reality of human presence. When the space-time dimensions have disappeared, it would still be possible to exist for another person. The risen Christ, now freed from the limitations of space and time, still exists for us and for each human person. Christ is constantly present to us because of the fact that he exists humanly for us.

If the incarnation means anything, it must mean that the Son of God sought identification with man. Through becoming man he became a member of the human race to draw it to unity with the Father. The incarnation, then, is the realization of the most basic law of love and friendship—to find identity with the beloved.

The most basic element in love is the process of identification with the other per-

son. Love demands that two persons begin
to consider each an extension of the other.
This the Word of God has done in becoming human. Not only did he take on the human condition, but also existed for no other
purpose than for his fellow man. He had no
reason to be man other than to live his
humanity for us.

As a creative being a person has an orientation to fulfillment. Therefore, when I
identify with some one, when I choose another to be my friend, his good becomes my
good. Also, when I place myself in his position and consider what is good for him,
I really see what is good for myself. My own
identification as a drive toward fulfillment
now includes another person. Because the
incarnation is directed to the whole human
race, the mystery of Christ's presence somehow touches all men.

If, then, I identify with Christ (this is
what it means to be a christian), I make
what is good for him my own good. I become
like him, for my fulfillment is his fulfillment.
Therefore, since Christ is present only for
men, my existence must be his mission. I,

then, as a christian, must have at heart the
desire to unify all men in community since
this is Christ's identity. He is human because
of his presence to men, his giving of himself
to men; I must be present to men and give
myself to others.

Christ's presence in the eucharist is the
ultimate expression of my union with him and
with my fellow man. It is the christian's celebration of the unity he already possesses and
a promise to bring that union to fulfillment.

> For God's Word, by whom all things were
> made, was himself made flesh so that as per-
> fect man he might save all men and sum up
> all things in himself. The Lord is the goal of
> human history, the focal point of the longings
> of history and of civilization, the center of the
> human race, the joy of every heart, the answer
> to all its yearnings. He it is whom the Father
> raised from the dead, lifted on high and sta-
> tioned at his right hand, making him judge
> of the living and the dead. Enlivened and
> united in his Spirit, we journey toward the
> consummation of human history, one which
> fully accords with the counsel of God's love:
> "To re-establish all things in Christ, both those
> in the heavens and those on the earth" (Eph.
> 1:10). (*Pastoral Constitution on the Church in
> the Modern World*, n. 45)

DISCUSSION QUESTIONS

1. What trends can be seen which would indicate that the world is growing toward a community of mankind? What trends are working against this effort?

2. What is community? How do your group, your family, and your friends form a community? What qualities should be found in a community?

3. Why does the christian have an obligation to join the sweep toward world-wide community? What can you as a christian offer this movement?

4. How is one person present to another person? How does a casual relationship differ from a friendship? How does our friendship with one another help us to understand the incarnation?

5. How is the union we already possess celebrated in the eucharist? Why should participation in the eucharist inspire us to seek the community of mankind?

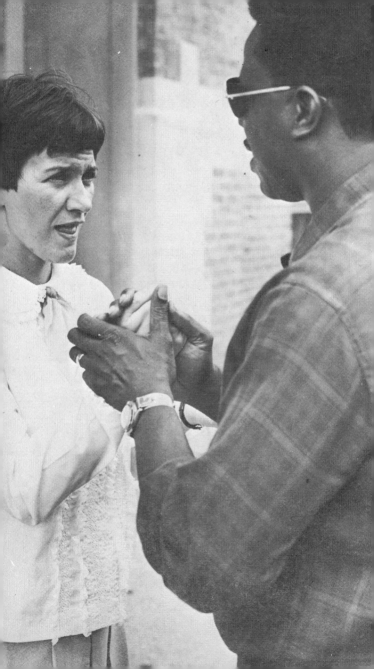

TWO

The Presence of Christ among Men

THE EUCHARIST IS the supreme expression of man's unity with Christ and with his fellow man. However, his presence in the eucharist is the culmination of his presence among his believers in other modes. How does the reality of Christ's presence touch the church, the community of faith? Obviously, such a discussion is based on the supposition of faith. The scriptural data is quite clear that the entire human career of Jesus, through the years of his earthly life and his risen life, is a self-giving to men. While there is only one Christ who is present to christians, the modes of his presence are many.

Christ is present to his community of faith because he shares with them his own redemptive mission and activity. This mystery of Christ's priesthood is witnessed to by all christians. There is only one priesthood and only one redemptive mission, which is

the priesthood and the mission of Christ.
Each christian shares in them in his own
way and in his own times. Just as the Father
sent Christ and worked in and through the
humanity of his Son, so the risen Christ continues his saving work through those who
believe in him.

The supreme and eternal priest, Christ Jesus,
since he wills to continue his witness and ser-
vice also through the laity, vivifies them in this
Spirit and increasingly urges them on to every
good and perfect work.
For besides intimately linking them to his
life and his mission, he also gives them a sharing in his priestly function of offering spiritual
worship for the glory of God and the salvation
of men. (*Dogmatic Constitution on the
Church*, n. 34)

This presence of Christ is directed to the
community of faith. Each individual christian shares in it through baptism. While it is
true to say that each christian brings the
reality of Christ to daily living, this must not
be understood in an individualistic sense.
Christ is in the people of God, the community
of believers. It is the whole christian community that is the object of the priestly

presence of Christ. This presence of Christ will become more intense in proportion to the christian community's conscious and generous opening of itself to the priestly mission.

Since Christ shares with his followers his redemptive mission, he also shares with them his human destiny. This destiny is the unending union with his Father. The risen Christ carries on the work of fulfilling his destiny by acting through the church, which is his body and sacrament. Those who share Christ's priesthood and his mission are linked with him in this destiny to union with the Father.

In addition to his priestly presence, Christ is also present to christians by sharing with them his own personal identity. Just as in genuine friendship each person strives to give himself to the other, so also Christ, who is bound to us in love, shares with us his own identity. The believer becomes the alter ego of Christ.

In deep friendship we strive to share our identity by communicating to another person the insights, the motivation, the experiences by which we identify ourselves. It is to the extent that a friend makes these bases of our self-identity his own, that he can identify with us. The most profound root of Christ's personal identity is his relationship with his Father. Christ is the Son, who gives to men a share in his own sonship. He does this by giving us his Father as our own. We can only begin to appreciate Christ's presence for us when we realize that we are sons of the Father. Christ in a very real sense is the first-born of many children, because through Christ's love for men, his Father is our own. Because Christ shares his identity with us, we become sons of God; brothers of one another.

The presence of Christ which the christian community possesses through sharing in his priesthood and sonship may seem to have little bearing on our experience. But if we examine this from the viewpoint of the presence of Christ in faith, we will be brought into closer contact with our christian experience.

Here again we must draw upon our knowledge of friendship. When I accept a person as my friend I come to know that person more and more. I allow him to occupy my consciousness. As the friendship deepens, my friend truly begins to "dwell within me." He is with me even when distance separates us.

The gospel of St. John permits us to apply the laws of friendship to our relationship with Christ. "If any one loves me, my Father will love him, and we will come and make our abode with him" (Jn. 14:23). And St. Paul prays for christians "that Christ may dwell by love in your hearts." This is the human side of making Christ's presence to us possible. Presence is constituted by being for another; but one can only be for another effectively if that other person accepts this offer of friendship.

Christian faith is meant to be a consciousness of the reality of the presence of the risen Christ. It is an awareness of him, who is our brother and our friend, an awareness that is different from any other. The reason why it is different is that it does not have a basis in sensible experience. This awareness is not an illusion. It has dominated the consciousness of men and women down through the ages and has inspired them to greatness.

When such an awareness of Christ's living reality is found in the community of faith, their faith-consciousness is truly the dwelling place of Christ in the world. For christians then bear the presence of Christ in their attitudes and activity.

Christ's presence to us requires our openness to him in faith, the total personal acceptance of Christ. To believe in Christ is not only to accept the fact that he is, it is to accept him as being *for us*. It is to allow him to be effectively present to us.

Christ's presence to christians—by their sharing his mission and sonship, consciously accepted in faith—is meant to be a force for transforming their lives and the lives of the men with whom the christian meets, lives and works. If christians live in the awareness of the relationship they bear to Christ, this will inevitably change their attitudes toward people. They will reverence others, be deeply concerned for their genuine human welfare, empathize with them in their sorrows, devote themselves to improving the world. In this way, Christ himself will be working to redeem the lives of all men through the impact he makes through the faith of christians.

Faith is unquestionably the key to the presence of Christ in our human lives, and, therefore, the key to the transforming and redeeming power of Christ in our midst. This may seem like a shaky foundation on which to build one's life. Christian life is indeed a risk. Yet, how do we know our christian faith is not an illusion? How do we know that Christ really exists as risen Lord? that Christ is actively present to us in our lives? The answer may sound naïve, but the only one that can be given is: because he tells us so. To justify this answer, we must look at the fourth mode of Christ's presence to us, his presence through communication with us.

If human beings want to be present to one another it is absolutely basic and essential that they communicate with one another. By word, by gesture, a smile, kindness, we make clear to another person that we are interested in him. Without such communication, a community and friendship could never be established. The constant deepening of communication is a sign that a friendship is growing. So also, the presence of Christ to us in faith must be rooted in some form of personal dialogue with Christ. Even though our faith is in many ways an ultimate risk, nonetheless, communication between Christ and ourselves is necessary.

The earthly career of Jesus is an important element in this communication. During his earthly existence Jesus communicated in a perceptible human form with his disciples and his contemporaries. Through this historical communication, the essence of his teaching has come down to us through the witness of the early christians. This communication makes it possible for us to respond in our thought and life to the message of Jesus. However, if our response to Christ could be no more than such a dialogue with the Jesus of history, we would not be involved in the kind of communication required for friendship. The impact of the Jesus of history would be present to us. But this is quite different from the presence of the risen Christ now.

So often we speak of Christ communicating to us through one another, through scriptures, and through the sacraments. Even though it is difficult we must reflect upon these and come to realize the psychological impact these modes of presence have. Experientially these three modes are intertwined. The one that seems to be most basic is Christ's speaking to us in one another.

We have treated of Christ's speaking to us in one another when we discussed the witness the believing christian gives his faith. This witness finds its most important function within the christian community itself. Anyone who searches for the criterion of faith will discover that he is dependent upon the faith of his fellow christians. The reality of Christ's presence, for most of us, came from our parents, was re-enforced by our teachers and finds support in our friends. The faith in the lives of those we love has been a critically important basis for our own judgment of faith. This is not merely a matter of the beginnings of faith; throughout the years of growth as a christian, Christ's presence in my fellow believers continues to speak to me. Each christian (and in some sense every human being) is a "word" of Christ to me, a challenge to which I must respond.

The "word" of Christ comes to me, for example, through christian love. A christian

is not identical with Christ. But because
Christ is present to the christian, he is loving
others in him and through him. The christian
sees other men and knows that Christ loves
them, and this intensifies the love he himself
has for them. Insofar as the christian chooses
to extend his genuine love to others, the love
of Christ will reach others and redeem them.

It is not just the faith of the individual
christian that is meant to be a word of Christ;
the communal faith of the church bears the
presence of Christ to me. To dialogue with
Christ and deepen my awareness of his presence in my life I must learn to listen to the
developing faith in the church as a whole.

From the earliest days of the church, christians have testified to one another the presence of Christ. The first generation enjoyed
a special benefit, however; their immediate
experience of Christ was the basis of their
faith. The infant church gathered the record
of Christ's teaching and the witness of the
apostles in the New Testament. Each succeeding generation of Christians has spoken
its faith, not just by using its own language
but also by the reading of scripture. In this

way Christ continues to speak through his
apostles during all the centuries of the life
of the church.

Scripture is the word of God, not just a
word about God. Scripture is sacramental.
When it is proclaimed in a christian community, it expresses the mind of Christ as he
is present in the faith of the community. Also,
it expresses the faith of the christian today
and the continuing faith of the historical
church. In responding to the word of the
bible, the christian is in dialogue both with
the community of faith and with Christ himself.

Much the same kind of communication between christians and the risen Christ is established in the celebration of the sacraments.
While scripture is the spoken word, the sacraments are enacted word. Everything about a
sacrament, not just the spoken word, is meant
to convey meaning to the community of
believers. The purpose of the sacraments is
to communicate understanding in faith to
the christian.

Sacraments speak for Christ because he is
the one acting. He acts through the agency

of the church which is his body. It is the very
action then that we christians carry out in the
sacraments which is the action of Christ, for
we are acting as his body. What we are
doing he is doing in and through us. In order
to understand what Christ is saying in these
actions, we must attend to what we are doing.
Only if a sacrament is this kind of response
to Christ's communication with us will it become an occasion for deepening Christ's presence to us in faith.

The various modes of Christ's presence
interact and have their zenith in the action
of the eucharist. When christians gather to
offer the mass, Christ is already present in
their midst because he is sharing with them
his priesthood. In virtue of this priesthood
the community of christians proceeds to sacrificial worship. As the word of scriptures is
proclaimed to them, they are brought closer
into union with the mind of Christ who is
speaking to them. Through this their personal
relationships to him deepen, his personal
presence to them is made more profound.
Christ is present in and through the words
he speaks.

When men wish to communicate with one

another, mere words are not enough. We need and search for other signs to convey the meaning that we wish to convey. This is what Christ does in the eucharistic action. To convey the incredible reality of his love for his disciples and believers, Christ uses the sign values of both food and the human body, combining them in the mystery we designate traditionally by the term "transubstantiation." Christ is immediately present to the species, that is, he is immediately present to the aspects of bread and wine that can carry significance. The bread and wine are a word which makes it possible for Christ to be deeply present to the faith of the assembled christian community. Christ's presence to the eucharistic species cannot be understood in isolation. The eucharistic presence has reality and meaning only as part of the process of communication by which he is present in faith to the christian.

The eucharistic dialogue between Christ and the christians who are participating in the action comes to its fulfillment in the reception of the body of Christ. Communion is the goal of community and the fulfillment of presence. While this eucharistic intensification of Christ's presence is meant to be the high point in our christian experience of faith, it is by no means the exclusive occasion of Christ's presence. Christ continues to be present to those who have shared in the eucharist when they have dispersed to their various tasks.

This presence of Christ in the eucharist is, therefore, and can be, the force that urges us to unity. From one point of view it is already the fulfillment of unity. From another point of view it urges on to unity. It gives christians a sense of belonging, of sharing, of being united. The eucharist, as the intensification of Christ's presence among us, gives an experience of community and communion.

This experience does not allow the christian to be possessive of its effect, but pushes him to share this community and communion with other men. The eucharist urges the christian to exercise his priesthood in the world and to work so that Christ will be in all. The *Constitution on the Sacred Liturgy* shows how liturgical celebrations unite the various presences of Christ.

To accomplish so great a work, Christ is always present in his church, especially in her liturgical celebrations. He is present in the sacrifice of the mass, not only in the person of his minister, "the same now offering, through the ministry of priests, who formerly offered himself on the cross," but especially under the eucharistic species. By his power he is present in the sacraments, so that when a man baptizes it is really Christ himself who baptizes. He is present in his word, since it is he himself who speaks when the holy scriptures are read in the church. He is present, lastly, when the church prays and sings, for he promised: "Where two or three are gathered together in my name, there am I in the midst of them" (Mt. 18:20) (n. 7).

Just as the incarnation was the beginning of Christ's unity with men and their world, so also the christian now sees that that world must be brought into full union with Christ. Without Christ human life is meaningless.

DISCUSSION QUESTIONS

1. How do christians make Christ present by their activity? What is the priestly function of Christ in which each one of us shares? By sharing in the activity of Christ how do we become like him?

2. How does our faith in one another foster friendship? What happens to us the more we develop our love for one another? What takes place in us if we allow our faith and love in Christ to grow?

3. How does Christ communicate with us? How is it possible for Christ to be present to us in others? How was Christ first made present to us? How does this witness of others influence us daily?

4. What role do the scriptures play in making Christ present to us? In what sense are they Christ speaking to me today?

5. Why is the eucharist the zenith of all the various ways in which Christ is present? What does Christ convey in the eucharist? Why is communion important to complete the eucharistic action?

THREE

Christ's Action in
the Eucharist

IN THE PREVIOUS chapter we discussed the eucharist as the mystery of presence, of how the eucharist is the summit of Christ's various presences among men. But there is more involved in the eucharist than Christ's presence to us. There is also Christ's action, the mystery of Christ's redemptive acts. There is a re-enactment of what Christ did at the last supper and calvary. This must not be understood, however, as something completed in the past. It is not merely a recalling of the past. The actions of Christ, insofar as they are represented in the eucharist, continue to take place because Christ the risen Lord is present to us, and continues to exist for us.

There is a recollection or commemoration or even representation in religious rituals throughout the world and throughout history. If the christian does not understand the christian meaning of mystery, it would seem that

christianity is no different from some ancient
"mystery" religions. Even though twenty
years ago it would have been fashionable to
say there was little difference in the rituals
of christianity and other religions, study and
scholarship have pointed out that there are
specific differences. Even between the Old
Testament rituals and christian commemoration, there are profound differences.

In the christian sense, mystery does not
essentially mean something which is hidden.
Mystery in the christian sense means something revealed. While in many ancient religions mystery meant the occult, christian
mystery manifests. Mystery, then, should
mean to us a gradual process by which Christ
is revealed as what he was and who he is.
There is a depth of understanding involved
here. Although the christian mysteries reveal
Christ and the rituals reveal his action, they
are so profound that we will never compre-
hend them totally. Perhaps the best explanation of this is the person himself. No person
is completely comprehensible, not even to
himself. If this is true on the human level,
there is an even greater incomprehensibility,

on our own part, of a divine person and his actions. This is the christian mystery and ritual. While they reveal they can never lay bare the total reality involved.

In the Old Testament there is already present a distinctive element of commemoration in ritual actions. The Jewish people had undergone an actual historical experience which they saw as something carried on by their God; Yahweh had allowed them to pass from slavery in Egypt to freedom. This was to be only the beginning of a series of actual historical occurrences which, in faith, they saw as the direct intervention of God. Here is something drastically different from other ancient religions. In other religions the normal course of events in society, in nature, or some tragic event like a flood or a storm is explained in some sort of imaginative description, a myth.

For Israel a mystery is actually a commemoration of a datable historical event. The way the Jews see the event is rather mystic; they draw upon their own oriental traditions to interpret the event, but nonetheless, they are referring to an event in their history.

They did cross the waters in Exodus; they did wander in the desert; they did finally come into the Promised Land; they were ruled by kings in preference to God; they did undergo exile in Babylon and were allowed to return.

This element of actual reference to an historic event is the characteristic note of the Old Testament rituals. There is also another characteristic which must not be allowed to go unnoticed. The celebration of the Passover, for example, was not just a commemorating of the fact year after year that their fathers had come out of the land of Egypt. The celebration of this ritual was also an entering on their part into the same dispensation with God which began in the Passover. The Passover was not in the past; the Jews were conscious of something still happening. The process which had its antecedent in history was still continuing. In the recollection of how the dispensation with God began, they gave themselves the opportunity to enter into a relationship with God. Therefore, the Passover ritual was a commemoration, and at the same time a personal entrance into the same mystery.

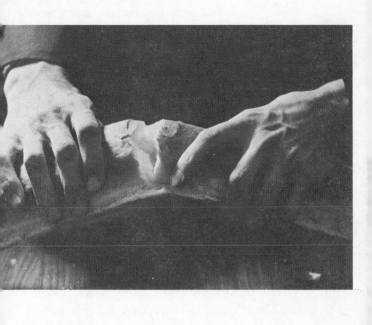

In the christian era at the beginning of the church, the christian rituals seem to have very much the same character. But there is something different. When the christians gathered at eucharist, they gathered for a christian assembly. Not only are they recollecting the fact that Christ came, lived in their midst, suffered and died, and on the night before he died said, "This is my body" and "This is my blood." They are commemorating those events, but they are also conscious that this is a continuation of what began there. What is different now is that what took place then is taking place now.

This attitude is expressed in the fourth Eucharistic Prayer:

> Father, we now celebrate this memorial of our redemption. We recall Christ's death, his descent among the dead, his resurrection, and his ascension to your right hand; and, looking forward to his coming in glory, we offer you his body and blood, the acceptable sacrifice which brings salvation to the whole world.

The "taking place now" is unique to the christian idea of commemoration, as opposed to the commemorative assemblies of other religious groups. The mystery is actually taking place *now*. Representation does not simply mean a recalling, recollecting, seeing the present implications of what happened. The mystery is actually taking place for the christian. Christ is still performing his redeeming action. The significance of the mystery is not simply in what we are doing now. The significance is not in that the meaning of the mystery is present now and still has an impact on us. The mystery-action itself is taking place here. This is what is meant by the presence of the mystery of Christ which we perform in the eucharist.

It is not as if we are acting out the eucharistic action as the christian community, and, behind this screen, there is mysteriously contained the mystery-action. Our action of the eucharist is the mystery-action. We who are performing the action are the mystery, not by ourselves, but precisely because Christ is in our midst. And Christ is performing his action in our midst. What Christ is performing through us is not historically discrete from that which took place the night before he died nor from Calvary. Also, the eucharistic action is not discrete from the mystery of the resurrection, because he is the risen Christ here in our midst. This is the event celebrated.

How can these events really be present? In our celebration of the eucharist there is present now the action of the redemption, the last supper, Christ's death and resurrection. By saying that everything significant in Christ's death and resurrection is present in the eucharist, we are really defining what is meant by sacrament. The action of Christ in the eucharist is a sacrament, a sign which points to something else, with respect to the last supper, death and resurrection. The celebration of the eucharist points to all that happened and its meaning in relation to our redemption. Also, all the meaningfulness, all the significance of the entire context of revelation prior to the last supper is also contained here. All of biblical theology, all the events of God's action over the centuries is contained in a supremely complex form in the rite which is the eucharist.

The first level of meaning, then, in the
eucharist, is the historical significance of
the events of Christ's life for our redemption.
This is not to be understood as a past event,
but that Christ even now redeems us. This
is as far as some protestant confessions would
go in their understanding of the eucharist.
They believe that all the meaning of the
eucharist is here in the recalling of the major
events of Christ's life and their impact on the
individual. As they come to understand the
significance of everything that God has been
saying by way of word, the eucharist becomes the supreme word—all converges in
the eucharist.

But there is another level in which everything that happened on Calvary is present.
This is the level of the human consciousness
of Christ. Christ is performing the eucharist
action in our midst as an integral human
being. As such he has a memory and has the
experience of his passover.

Just as you and I at this particular moment
contain in our psychology a history of everything that we have done, so Christ *contains*
his total human experience. Any experience

that we have at this given moment is conditioned by what we have been, have said or done. We do not approach anything neutrally. Up to this point we are the accumulation of an entire life experience. In the supernatural order, this is the theology of the development of merit. In our lifetime we build toward the last moment when, as we pass into the next life, we have established our self-identification as this person.

Christ, also, cannot divorce himself from the fact that he passed through death into risen life. For him, risen life which is now his existence cannot mean anything different than the final stage of his earthly life, which is his passover. The mystery of Christ's redeeming us is not just his death; it is the entire history of his human life which led him to the final moment and is his risen life. It is the new exodus, the passing over, which is the paschal mystery. The resurrection is the term of the process of passing through death. The whole human experience of Christ is operative in our midst.

The whole human consciousness of Christ which underlies the mystery of the eucharistic action of the mass is a consciousness in which death and everything that preceded it are present still. When the risen Christ speaks as he does through his signs in the eucharist, he is speaking of the fact that he is in this final stage which necessitated passing through death. Even in his human experience now, he is in a completely triumphant state, the outcome of his life on earth. Therefore, when we enter into his action in the human consciousness of Christ, we enter all the mysteries of his life. This is what is done in living the liturgical year. We live through all the various mysteries and we reflect on them.

As we pass through these mysteries we come to understand various facets of the present human consciousness of Christ and of what he is saying to us in his action. Our meditation is not essentially upon the multiplication of the loaves, the storm at sea, this or that parable, but upon the mystery action of the mass itself.

Therefore, the second level of understanding the eucharist mystery is a deepened, broadened understanding of the mind of Christ so that when we come to participate in the eucharist we can join our mentality to Christ's.

The third, and perhaps the most important level of understanding the eucharist, is the heart of the action that is present. What took place at the last supper and at Calvary in the memory of Christ is important, but it is a residue, so to speak. When we perform an action personally, the important part of the action is not the immediately visible, the immediately tangible, the external element. When I perform an external act, what is really important is the spiritual dimension of it; my consciousness, my intention, my emotional response, my imaginative life at that moment. This is the portion of the action in which I am involved as a person. This aspect makes me more or less a person. It is this portion of what Christ did, beginning with the supper and carried through on Calvary, which is redemptive. The very heart of the action of Christ is not, as it were, the external translation. What was really the heart of the redemptive portion was Christ's awareness, his consciousness, his free and loving acceptance of his suffering as redemptive.

This consciousness begins in formal sacrificial context at the last supper. This moment of his conscious acceptance of his death is now put in a formal public setting. The external manifestation of that acceptance is the ritual use of the bread and the wine in the context of the paschal situation. Therefore, the paschal meal is the external manifestation of the internal attitude of Christ. The new covenant is the acceptance of Christ as shared in the eucharist. This action of Christ in the eucharist is one continuing act of consciousness, unbroken and indistinguishable, an action which continues now straight through to the agony in the garden, the actual condemnation, the moment of death, and into the new life.

What Christ tells us through the externals of the mass is that the center of the redeeming action is still going on at the present moment. Christ is not saying anything different now from what he said at the last supper. We use the same external symbolism, because another external symbolism would not make present this identical action. It does not seem to be possible to use other forms

of food which, perhaps, are more common to our culture. The reason is that God is not just feeding us, but is also giving us life. What is signified in the eucharist is the presence of that very identical life-giving action which was the action at the last supper, the action of Calvary, the action of Christ accepting risen life. Christ accepted passage from this life into new life in order to give a new life to us. Christ chose this passage; it did not just happen. "I lay down my life, and I take it up again."

Every time we celebrate the eucharist, this same awareness, this same consciousness is present. Christ is present in this precise act of accepting his concrete situation in risen life in order to share it with us. This is what St. Paul means when he says: "As often as you shall eat the body and drink the blood, you show forth the death of the lord until he comes." In the eucharist, Christ speaks instrumentally through us. We speak it: Christ speaks it. The mystery of the whole Christ is present, the mystery of Christ redeeming in our midst through the church. The mystery that is spoken is the mystery of Christ and the mystery of the church. They are one mystery expressed in the eucharist action. Therefore, the mystery that is present is ourselves.

In the mass the christian stands up to identify himself with the mystery of death and resurrection. We become involved. In each individual's life, and in the life of the church, there must be a constant accepting of the same decision that Christ made. There must be a passing from the past into the future, of dying to what was and moving into what is to be. This is not just a metaphor or poetry. This constant passing from death to life is a fundamental experience of human life. Many people think that the past is something solid, whereas in fact it is gone, it will not be again. And the future has not come. All of us are on a sharp edge that is moving from the past to the future. Even the present cannot be grasped; by the time you have finished reading this sentence, the time you began reading it is gone. This is what it means to be a creature. But the christian knows that the future is solid. The future is clearly present in the eucharist because the risen Christ is in the fulfillment of christian life. The christian moves into the mystery of what Christ already is.

We are assured of this in the seventeenth chapter of John's gospel. In that text Christ is described as already in his redemptive mystery. He has already performed the act of the last supper and is moving into its fulfillment. He turns to his Father and prays: "I pray, Father, that where I am these may also be." That is the fundamental priestly attitude of Christ. The process of Christ in human history is one of drawing men toward himself, toward risen life. He draws each one of us individually in our own life experience this way, but he also draws the corporate existence of the church in this direction. In this way there is manifest a whole prospect of the christian community as a community and as individuals visibly marching toward fulfillment in the resurrection of Christ.

This is the mystery that is taking place in the eucharist. The resurrection of Christ is not a static thing as if Christ had reached his glory and now his work is done. He told his apostles: "I have worked until now and my

Father works." Christ continues to work through the dynamics of his resurrection. This is the mystery of Christ that we re-present; we make it present again because we are part of it. The action of the eucharist, then, is the commemorating of something precisely by making it now present. All the significance of what Christ said and did, all the significance of the Old Testament, all the significance of the natural world is present in the eucharist. There is a complex sacramentality in our celebration of the eucharist. This is expressed in the fourth eucharistic prayer:

> Father, we acknowledge your greatness: all your actions show your wisdom and love. You formed man in you own likeness and set him over the whole world to serve you, his creator, and to rule over all creatures. Even when he disobeyed you and lost your friendship you did not abandon him to the power of death, but helped all men to seek and find you. Again and again you offered a covenant to man, and through the prophets taught him to hope for salvation.

The very event we are celebrating in the eucharist is present within ourselves. This is the most important aspect of understanding the eucharist. Only if the presence of the eucharist within ourselves begins to shine through do we begin to appreciate how the mystery of redemption is incarnated in culture.

In the next chapter we must discuss the eucharist as redemption. Unless we realize the redeeming action that is present, we develop the mentality that by sharing in the eucharist we are drawing upon the account of Christ's merits. Redemption is not something that was done, but is continuing. If we can understand this we have an immediate response to the person in the eucharist. We do not pray to the Christ on the cross two thousand years ago, but to the Christ present now who is still fully conscious of the fact of fully accepting me. I relate to Christ today and this controls my whole response to him.

DISCUSSION QUESTIONS

1. What is the meaning of "mystery" for christians? How does this differ from mere commemoration or recalling? How is the founda-

tion of the christian's understanding of mystery already found in the Old Testament?

2. In what way are the redemptive actions of Christ taking place now? How is the eucharist the same celebration that took place twenty centuries ago?

3. Discuss the various levels of meaning expressed in the eucharist, and how we share in them.

4. What should be the attitude of each christian as he participates in the action of the eucharist? How is the offering, death, and resurrection being realized in our life?

5. Can we live the eucharistic action? How would this be done in our daily lives?

FOUR

The Eucharist as Redemption

THERE ARE SO MANY aspects of the eucharist which could be treated, because once you delve into the meaning of this sacrament, you begin to see that its theology is co-extensive with christianity. Everything that the church does either flows toward or from this action. One of the most important aspects is, of course, what should we get out of the eucharist? What is the eucharist really doing for people? When you answer that the eucharist is redemption, is this an exterior process that is going on or is it something that we can constantly and progressively participate in? If the eucharist is a source of renewal, how can we enter more profoundly into this process?

To understand what the eucharist can do for us, it is important to understand what redemption is. Redemption is not something that happened; it is something that is going on now. Christ's redeeming of the human race is a continuing process precisely because the very heart of his redeeming action is his internal consciousness and decision and love. Christ's acceptance of the mysteries of the passover is the redeeming power at work in our times.

We might look at the process of redemption as the process of re-ordering. The finality which was meant to exist in the individual man and in man's social existence was thwarted and diverted by sin. The origins of this deviation rest in original sin, but personal sin down through history also has infected the individual, the community, mankind. Therefore, whatever God does cannot be simply an unimpeded thrust toward perfection. His work in man can direct man toward his destiny by correcting this perversion, which is a disorder. Redemption is the conquering of the disorder in the individual, in society, in the world-community.

Redemption, then, becomes the process of re-establishing in man the order which should prevail. This must be accomplished essentially with man as person. Man as person is

directed in his power of knowing and in his love and his freedom toward the expression of himself by confronting reality as it is, and by opening up to personal being, and above all the three Divine Persons. By moving in this direction, by opening ourselves as persons in knowing and loving, by committing ourselves to this in trust, we fulfill ourselves. Through this we become deeply personal and reach union with the Divine Persons, our destiny.

Redeeming becomes a question of reconstructing the person, of rebuilding him, of reorienting him. Grace is the re-orientation of the person. In causing grace in us, Christ is re-shaping us; he is imprinting on us his own humanity and his own divine personality. The precise orientation that we have as persons in redemption is that our whole person says, "I acknowledge being a son of this Father." The re-direction of ourselves back towards God the Father in union with Christ constitutes our redemption.

The eucharist is the situation of reconciliation. It is the celebration of the reconciliation which has taken place. The sacraments of baptism and penance make reconciliation possible, but the eucharist perfects it. The eucharist stands in relation to peace as the feast in the parable of the prodigal son. The father gives the feast for his erring son to celebrate his reconciliation with him. The externals of the mass make quite clear that the eucharist is the reconciliation between the heavenly Father and sinful man.

In what way is redemption achieved in the sacrifice of the mass? The mass, first of all, is a dialogue, a situation of word and response. In the mass the mystery of the Father's love, made concrete by sending his Son Incarnate, is expressed, and the mystery of that Son's love is response. The Son's love is given at the expense of having to encounter death in order to give life to men. In terms of the reality of dialogue, there is given to us the promise of fulfillment of life. We are presented with our own identification as christians at this particular moment in history, pertaining to this precise christian community, with these precise apostolic demands upon us, because we find ourselves here and now in this place and time. The mass is a challenge to confront reality by accepting it.

This is the vision of human life that is presented to us in the mass. If we respond to it, if we profess our faith, which the act of the mass should be, we are taking our powers of consciousness and are directing them in union with Christ toward the reality which is before us. We are no longer afraid to look at it as we do in sin. We are not turning away from that which is meant to be the goal of this particular power, the power of God. Because of that, the very action we are performing in the sacrifice of the mass is the directing of ourselves contrary to what would be the deviations of sin in us. We do not do this by ourselves. In the sacrifice of the mass, as we say "Father," we do it through the Spirit as Paul tells us in Galatians. Because the Spirit dwells in us we are able to cry out "Abba, Father." We do not just decide to do this; we do it because God is working in us. God is redeeming us and we are redeeming ourselves.

Redemption depends on the person. God cannot redeem a person who will not redeem himself. Our action in the mass is our own redemption. We are redeeming ourselves, but

we are doing it only because the divine action
is working in us, making it possible for us to
redeem ourselves.

I cannot permit my consciousness to ad-
vance toward that difficult and fear-filled
process of discovering reality unless I have
that personal security which comes from loving and being loved. An insecure person cannot go out and exercise love and face reality.
He walls himself off from it. Only in the context of deep personal security, grounded in
friendship, love, and a sense of belonging, is
a person able to do this. In the mass there
must be also, for our redemption, a contact
of integral and radical commitment in love.
Such a response is possible because the precise reality of which the mass speaks is that
of a deep and personal love directed toward
us. An infinitely loving Father, because he
loves us, sends his Son into our midst so that
his love might be a sacrament, the translation, the contact point for us with this profound mystery.

Whenever love is presented it is a challenge. Love challenges our response. This is
the reason why men, once they understand

the eucharist, can no longer remain neutral to this gift. In the past as well as in the present, many christians have been allowed to remain neutral because they have not understood or do not understand the eucharist. In other human experiences, they encounter the challenge and the demands of a response. A person comes into your life, a person who genuinely loves you. You cannot just let the situation stand, you must make a response; you say "yes" or "no" to the love offered. This is what God expects in the eucharist. The Book of Revelations says: "Because you are neither hot nor cold I will vomit you out of my mouth." The eucharist does not allow the christian to be anything but hot or cold. The christian must either accept or reject it. The christian must love.

The essence of sin is to reject love. The most radical element in sin is the refusal to love: to love one's self, to love others, to love God. The eucharist challenges us in all three. We must love ourselves, we must love the community associated with us and all men, and we must love the three Divine Persons. This is what the action in the mass demands.

As we continually participate in the eucharist and attempt feebly, patiently, to open our person to God and really to confront the Three Loves, the tendency toward sin reverses itself. If the essence of sin is essentially the negation of love, then the act of loving tears at the very root of sin. Love reverses the process and, as we grow in love, sin is rooted out of us. From our experience we learn that love is the most fulfilling of experiences even though at times it can be painful. As we begin to grasp that the eucharist is the presence of a love that never fails, we respond to it more faithfully.

The eucharist is the context in which love never fails. If this becomes a reality in my life, my hope does not rest so much on the historical fact of Christ's resurrection. There is not something about Christ we trust, but a person we trust; Christ is our hope, as scripture says. What we trust is a person.

God is faithful, a characteristic repeatedly attributed to God in revelation. He is a God who keeps his promise. Having promised to love us and having taken pleasure in his Son who is in us in the Spirit, he will never retract

his word. This is the new and everlasting
covenant. Christ himself is the person who
epitomizes this in his incarnation. Through
this promise that is given us in a human way,
we have the security to love, to be involved.
We can risk loving.

Many are afraid to love, to open themselves
to others, because their faith is not in the
promise of God, in Christ, in the eucharist.
For them, it is too risky to love; they might
be rejected. After building one's life and self-
identity on another and then being rejected,
confidence is lost. The christian can risk his
love again, because the one he has identified
with is the risen Christ. There is no need
to lose one's identity as a christian. Therefore,
because of the confidence we have in our
identity with Christ, the reorientation process,
which is our redemption, can take place and
will take place.

Redemption in its fulfillment means mystery of union. Man's destiny is union with
the three Divine Persons in terms of identification with the Word Incarnate. Man was
made for such a union. There can be no other
ultimate fulfillment. Union with God as our

final redemption is something, however, of the next life. Christianity does not teach from an apocalyptic point of view in which the process of history becomes meaningless. From such a view, we would have only to wait for a cataclysm and stand by and watch it all. Then a new era would be established. Christianity meets life and the world head on, because it believes that the world to come grows out of the world which is.

In the same way, our redemption, our union with God, is on the way right now. Again, this can be seen in the eucharist. The eucharist is a mystery of union with God the Father, in and through Christ; it is the mystery of union with the christian community; and it is the mystery of union with Christ himself.

There are two rather important dimensions, two aspects of this mystery of union with Christ expressed in the eucharist. One type of union is the union of cooperation. That is to say that Christ is in our history, in our life, as priest. As already explained, we sha.e in that priesthood. With Christ we perform the priestly action of redeeming the world and

ourselves. Actively, therefore, we are caught up in this redeeming stream of activity.

The redeeming activity is not like two people walking together or involved in a project together. The image is more accurate if we consider Christ as working through us. Only because Christ is working through us can we accomplish our redemption. The unity experienced in redemption is a dynamic unification; it is unity in doing something. This accomplishment is, of course, the re-orientation of human thinking, human understanding, human emotion, human love and human freedom. This is the function of every christian and of the whole church.

When we participate in redemption, we bring ourselves in line with Christ. In order to be an instrument of the redemptive love of Christ, we must begin to love that way; in order to be an instrument of openness to mankind, we have to begin to think that way. St. Paul says: "Let this mind be in you, which is also in Christ Jesus." Only when there is this kind of openness of our personal living can there be this mystery of unification and an effective apostolate in the church.

This, then, is one kind of unity expressed in the eucharist which is closely related to the whole apostolic spirituality of the church. If we are looking for a spirituality which fits the apostolate, we would find it in identification with Christ in his redemption, a unification with Christ in the operative mystery of redemption.

This does not take place automatically. This identification is constant, must be acquired, and must be developed. If this identification with Christ is developed, each christian, when he is acting in the church, can be aware of the context, and this leads him into the moment of sacrifice. In the moment of sacrifice, we enter most profoundly into the heart of action in christianity. This brings Christ's own historical redeeming into our midst now.

There is a second type of union, which is not person working with person, but person meeting person, friend meeting friend. And this also is a function of the eucharist. We not only exercise our priesthood with Christ, but as a community we are the bride of Christ. We are the object of his transforming

love, and he is the object of our personal response. In the mass the invitation to friendship and our response is contained from beginning to end. It is this aspect of the eucharist which is celebrated most significantly in our reception of the body of Christ. Under this physical sign of a coming together of two persons, there is really a deep unification in love. A mutual indwelling takes place.

Unification in love is the mystery of which Christ spoke at the last supper, especially as found in St. John's gospel: "In my Father's house there are many mansions." Christ continues: "Dwell in me, and I in you." This type of union is asked for in the eucharist. When the redemptive work has at last been accomplished, when the exercise of the priesthood in re-orienting human life is no longer required, the fulfillment of re-orientation will take place in union.

The union we now possess is union in formation. The re-orientation is not complete; it is in progress. However, it is meant to terminate in final unification in profound personal identification with the three Divine Persons and the whole of redeemed mankind. This is the redeeming that takes place in the eucharist.

In order to undertake our share of the redemption, we must see where the eucharist takes us, what it expects of us, what it accomplishes. To prepare other men to share in the eucharist, in total unification, we must apply our understanding of the parable of the sower—the man who went out to sow the word of God in the hearts of men. How do we get well-prepared soil? What does it mean to get men ready to share in the eucharist? If we ourselves understand and experience the eucharist as conversion, the re-direction of free, loving, conscious life, we can prepare others for this unity. We must change our own vision of life to help others see another vision. This is the level of real participation in the mystery of the eucharist. If we understand that the totality of our life and person is involved, then can the eucharist be what it is meant to be—a sacrament.

DISCUSSION QUESTIONS

1. Why can the eucharist be considered redemptive? What does redemption mean? How is Christ's redemption at work today?

2. Discuss how we experience and can help others to experience redemption. Give concrete examples of how you have experienced redemption.

3. What is the vision of human life that the mass presents to us? How can we carry this vision into daily living? What assurance can this vision give us?

4. Why can we not remain neutral to the eucharist? Why is the eucharist the ultimate challenge to love?

5. How does the eucharist re-orientate our thinking, our emotion, and our freedom? How can this re-orientation bring about unity in ourselves, with our fellow man, and with God?

FIVE

The Eucharist as
Sacrifice

IN THE PREVIOUS chapters we discussed the eucharist as the mystery of presence, then pointed out that presence is not simply a question of Christ being there. The mystery of redemption is also there. Christ still continues his mysteries. As the christian participates in these mysteries of Christ, he is led to the moment of sacrifice, the heart of the action of christianity. It is important, therefore, to discuss the way in which the eucharist action of the mass is a sacrifice.

In order to understand sacrifice in the christian context, we must go back to the Old Testament notion of sacrifice to give us a fuller understanding of what Christ did at the last supper. When Christ performed an action of sacrifice, he did it as a human being. He sacrificed according to the understanding he had. As a Jew his understanding was that

of a believing Jew of that era. Therefore, to
understand the christian notion of sacrifice,
it is important to understand the notion of
sacrifice in the mind of Christ as he ap-
proached this act which would institute the
christian sacrificial system.

In the Old Testament there is really no
generic notion of sacrifice. Perhaps most common was the idea of gift or offering. The
various types of ritual sacrifice that the Jews
possessed were holocaust, peace offering, the
offering of the meal, the grain, sin and tres-
pass offerings. The precise type of ritual
action, the kind of action that we would
classify as sacrifice, which is involved in the
background for the eucharist action of Christ,
is the peace offering. It is the type of action
in which, for example, a sheep is killed, and
then it is sanctified, brought into contact with
the altar, and the blood used ritually. Then
the meal takes place in which the people and
God share.

The people eat their share of the meat in
a meal. God enters into the consuming of his
share through the fire which transforms his
portion into a sweet savor which comes from

the fatty portion of the animal. The Jews had
the notion, shared with other people of the
ancient world, that God, because he is
spiritual, does not eat meat, but smell is
something spiritual, and a sweet smell is
something God will appreciate. In the sacrifice of Abel, the savor went up to God and
was accepted, while Cain's did not rise; therefore, God did not join himself to the sacrifice
of Cain.

From the Jews comes the idea of sacrifice
as a meal eaten together. When people ate
together they were bound in some sort of an
alliance. This notion, which the Israelites
shared with other ancient peoples, involved
God directly with the community. God was
involved in the sacred meal and, therefore,
he was bound to the members of the community in a covenant. Through the sacred
meal God had committed himself to man. An
alliance, or pact, was formed in this way.
Therefore if men wanted to maintain union
with God, they would join themselves to
him in a meal. Since he is the source of life,
the ancients were anxious not to have their
God far away from them. This is the primitive

notion of the covenant meal that underlies the paschal meal of the Old Testament.

The paschal meal was a special type of this sacrifice in that the whole of the animal was eaten by the people. If anything was left over, it was then burned. This is the background of Christ coming to the last supper to institute the eucharistic sacrifice.

In the Old Testament sacrifice, the killing of the animal was not important. It had little or no significance as a ritual since anyone could do this if necessary. But the blood had to be preserved. The ritual use of the blood was a priestly action as was the offering. *Killing was necessary, but did not enter into the sacrificial concept.* The killing was only a preparation and not part of the sacrifice. This is important in the consideration of what the fire does to the gift that is brought.

Our modern interpretation of the sacrificial offering would be the recognition of the sovereignty of God through the *destruction* of the offering by fire. But this is a very questionable interpretation. It seems that the Old Testament Jew looked upon the consummation by fire not as a destruction but as a *transformation.* The very element that was used, fire, was an element considered proper to God. Fire was interpreted as the instrument that God uses to transform the offering into a state of being which is somehow in the same realm in which he exists. Sacrifice is not considered a question of destruction but a question of changing something into the realms of the divine through fire.

When Christ was at the last supper, he was in the context of sacrifice. That is why it is important to understand the action of the last supper as much more than a changing of bread and wine. The last supper is the situation of a paschal feast with its note of jubilation, with its note of triumph, with its note of hope and expectation of messianic salvation. Christ took this feast in its entirety and transformed it. And in the course of transforming the feast, he specifically transformed the two elements of bread and wine, food and drink. The transformation of these two nourishing elements takes place in the context of the whole feast. The supper involved a celebration of the exodus, which was the source of the sacrificial system of Israel.

From the Book of Leviticus, we learn much about the theology of sacrifices in the Old Testament. This book explains the sacrificial system as commemoration, continuing and deepening what had taken place in that first event which made the people Israel. Whenever the Jews assemble now for the paschal feast, there is always an atmosphere of the establishment of covenant in sacrifice. Christ, too, comes to us christians in this context.

Meal is not incidental to the sacrifice. The partaking of a sacred meal is a sacrificial action, and this is what Christ is doing in the last supper. He thereby extends the Old Testament sacrificial meal into the New Testament sacrificial meal. The apostles and Christ together are performing the sacrificial action in eating the meal. The transformation takes place in the participation in the changed bread and wine.

When we come to the eucharist, we must keep in mind that the mass as a meal is not merely poetic imagery. It is not a pietistic attitude which places people in the sentimental atmosphere of the last supper. Also, we should not forget that the total setting is

sacrificial and not just the consecration. The meal, the eating, is performing the sacrificial action. Therefore, when people go to communion they are performing a sacrificial action.

One of the most central aspects of sacrifice is the offering. The Jews, generation by generation, offered themselves in terms of the paschal meal. When Christ takes the context of this meal, he is saying that we should do more than offer ourselves in the context of the old covenant. Christ offers himself solemnly in the transformation of the bread and wine and the transformation of the Pasch into the new covenant. Christ puts himself apart for the New Pasch. He solemnly, ritually, enters upon this action, which is going into exile, crossing the waters of death, and entering the new promised land which is his risen life. He dedicates himself to this at the moment of the transformation of the bread and wine. So he established a new covenant in a new covenant sacrifice. The offering of himself is essentially what is involved in this moment of the sacrifice. The sacrifice of Christ as it begins with his apostles continues into the action of Calvary, without which the last supper would be meaningless. On Calvary the final setting aside of the victim takes place.

In every sacrifice, by a ritual gesture, something is taken out of the profane and set apart for the sacred. This begins early in the mass. We take ordinary bread and wine and we sanctify them by separating them from the profane. This is done by placing them on the altar stone. From this point forward, they are no longer just ordinary bread and wine, even before the consecration. The final setting aside comes from the very substance of the change.

This final setting aside of Christ as victim came when he passed out of our context of temporal existence into this new thing which is beyond life. The final setting aside of himself as victim once and for all comes in death. There are two moments in the sacrifice of Christ. One is the offering of himself as victim. Christ sets himself aside as sacred. This is signified by the external signs at the last supper sacramentally. The second moment is the actual physical experience of dying realistically on Calvary. But there is one sacrifice uniting both moments. In one moment Christ places himself before the Father as belonging totally to him; in the other, he fulfills physically this intention.

In Christ as victim, offered and sacrificed, one can see the whole process of the divine action of transforming the victim. Christ offers himself to the Father; the Father accepts the offering and transforms the victim in glory. The Father raises the Son from destruction and glorifies him. The transformation involved in sacrifice would not be present if there were not the completion of this offering in the resurrection. The resurrection, then, is essential for the sacrifice of Christ and the eucharist.

Therefore, Holy Thursday, Good Friday and Easter Sunday must have been as one action; Christ's sacrifice would not be complete if one of these had been missing. Without the last supper, there would not have been the public assertion of the sacrifice as a solemn ritual action. Without the last supper, we could not recognize the death of Christ as sacrificial. On Calvary the actual setting aside takes place definitively. In the resurrection, the transformation of the victim is achieved. Sacrifice is, therefore, a whole process through death into risen life.

The sacrifice of Christ does not make any sense apart from any one of these three elements. These three aspects really form one mystery of redemption. They form the new passover. This is our Christian sacrifice. What we do in the sacrifice of the mass is to allow ourselves to be the instruments of Christ as he offers himself to his Father. He is still offering himself to his Father in that act of interior consciousness and choice mentioned in the previous chapter. Christ still sets himself aside willingly, accepts completely this passing of temporal existence into new life. He accepts totally, gracefully his being made sacred by God.

Now he expresses this in and through us, because there would be no sacrifice in history unless there were a visible manifestation of it. To make that sacrifice an operative mystery in human life as it continues, Christ uses our instrumentality. We participate in all the acts of the mass. Christ is still offering his sacrifice in and through us. The entire

community offers Christ. How can this be done? We can do this because Christ is ours; he belongs to us. We were baptized and he identified himself with us; he made us his. He gave us himself, therefore, as a *friend and brother*. Because he is ours we can very literally and rightfully offer him to the Father. Christ is offering himself to the Father; we are offering him. Also, as we are offering ourselves, Christ is offering us to the Father.

What does our offering mean? If we follow the pattern of the meaning of Christ's own offering, our sacrifice would mean the setting aside of ourselves as something no longer belonging to profane affairs, but something offered for sanctification. We set ourselves apart for being made sacred, for being introduced into the realm in which God himself operates. This is as far as we can go as human beings. We come and offer ourselves to be transformed, to be set apart, to be given up. But the divine action has to enter here. The divine action comes precisely through the sacramentalism of the transubstantiation. This bread which we cannot make into Christ, God does; ourselves whom we cannot make into Christ, God does. So transformed now by the divine action, we can become victims, consecrated, belonging to God, dedicated. This is the most basic element in sacrifice—to make sacred.

God is the one who makes us sacred, but he does not do this contrary to our own free choice. For as one is viewing the mass as sacrifice, there are several elements that must be pointed out. What has led our thinking astray in the past is the idea of immolation. Undoubtedly, we can explain that there is an immolation in the eucharistic act. After all, the eucharist is the profound immolation of one accepting new life completely. However, if one looks for the shedding of blood, there is a problem. There is no immolation in this sense. What is central is an offering. It is the offering of the people; it is the offering of Christ; and each one offers himself as a gift to him. The offering is the essential aspect. We offer ourselves for transformation, for being made God-like. And only in being made God-like can we really offer ourselves.

Under the form of a meal eaten together with God we are bound into an irreversible bond, covenant, with him. We can prove faithless to this, but from God's point of view, the covenant is something we have entered into. Through the eucharistic meal there is a communion, an establishment of unity between Christ and his church, between Christ, the church and the Father, between men among themselves through the meal which is being shared together. This is the fundamental notion of the eucharist as being a sacrificial action.

Let us move to the meaning of victim. The basic idea involved is that the victim is the one to whom something is done. This sounds like something very passive, directly opposed to the points thus far made. To gratefully accept life, perfection, change, transformation from God is really what it means to be a victim. Therefore, I, as victim, am not like a stone that is changed; I am a personal being. Therefore, the most important element in accepting christian victimhood is the acceptance of the concrete reality of my life situation.

Christ is a victim, because he is a willing victim. And by accepting victimhood he has redeemed us. That is the very essence of what he did. He was accepting the precise role that was his in human history. He accepted all the elements of things being done to him, and as man there came to him life and sanctification. He had to acknowledge his receptivity. Where we have to accept being dependent— for it is clear that something is being done to us—is the point at which we pass through death into life. That is the most critical moment of having to accept the types of creature we are. However, in the human condition it is not just a question of accepting the fact of being a creature. To recognize that I am a creature to whom life is given is not enough.

We are in a christian era. The polarity of creature-creator shifts now to son-Father. Therefore, we are not just accepting creaturehood, but we are accepting sonship. Therefore, in the sacrifice of the mass, I am openly and really accepting all things given me by the Father. This is the real act of faith in God as the Father. I willingly accept my creaturely condition in a christian way when I admit that I am one who must exist by reception of all that I have and all that I am because of the Father. My victimhood be-

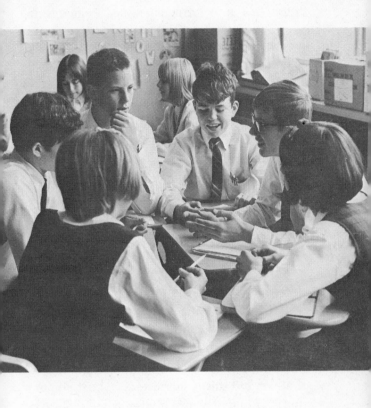

comes then, and only then, an active participation, and I am accepted as a personal
being.

The fundamental mentality of the christian,
which is the center of offering sacrifice, is the
acceptance of dependence. We turn to God
and allow him to redeem us. This is the active
part we play. We allow God to transform us
and re-order us. Therefore, we call the mass
the eucharist, because it is the action of giving thanks. And whenever we offer thanks to
someone, we accept the gift he offers us. God
offers us new life, and we thank him for it
by accepting that gift. Therefore, sacrifice
is not just enduring or accepting the will of
God passively. God is not interested in having
us suffer; he is interested in doing something
for us. In the mass we acknowledge God as
Father, and this is sacrifice. As Christ pointed
out: "If one of your children comes and asks
you for bread, would you give him a serpent?
If you would not give your child a serpent,
what about God, your Father." Our attitude,
then, in sacrifice is the acceptance of God as
Father, who transforms us into his sons.

The acknowledgement of this is the acceptance of victimhood. The acknowledgement of this is christian sacrifice. This is another way of saying that the mass is one word, and that is "Father." The theology of the mass and the liturgy is summed up in that one word. The eucharistic sacrifice is, in union with Christ, an acknowledgement on the part of the christian community of this corporate sonship. This is what the mass says, not just in an abstract and theoretical sense, but concretely so that we can accept it.

When we say "Father" we are opening ourselves up to the Father's transforming us by making us his sons. Once the divine action enters the mass, the community can turn to God the Father and acknowledge sonship. That is our offering of ourselves. We cannot do this without the action of God being present. In the last supper Christ accepts his sonship in a cultic and public fashion. He had acknowledged his sonship before, but in the eucharistic context he does this in an intense fashion. There is no greater way that he could ever have acknowledged his Father as Father than by being willing to

undergo the experience of death into the un-
known, which was risen life, and to do this
with perfect calm and peace and conviction
that his Father would raise him from the
dead. This he continues to do in the midst
of the christian community.

Any time we assemble for the sacrifice of
the mass, Christ is in our midst through our
human experience, our human offering of ourselves, continuing to say, in the diversified
fashion that we are, this word "Father." Taking the action of the mass as being sacrifice
and adding to this the meaning of victimhood, we have the supreme act of worship.
This is our acknowledgement as sons in sacrificial context of the Fatherhood of the Father
of our Lord Jesus Christ and also the Father
of all christians.

What does the christian offer in the mass?
What is his sacrifice? Vatican II answers:

> For all their works, prayers and apostolic
> endeavors, their ordinary married and family
> life, their occupations, their physical and
> mental relaxation, if carried out in the Spirit,
> and even the hardships of life, if patiently
> borne—all these become "spiritual sacrifices

acceptable to God through Jesus Christ." Together with the offering of the Lord's body, they are most fittingly offered in the celebration of the eucharist. Thus, as those everywhere who adore in holy activity, the laity consecrate the world itself to God. (*Dogmatic Constitution on the Church*, n. 34)

DISCUSSION QUESTIONS

1. Why is sacrifice considered to be the heart of christianity?

2. Why did the Jews consider sharing in a sacred meal to be a special union with God? How did this meal become a covenant?

3. How can sacrifice be understood as a transformation? How is this true in our daily lives? How is this true in our participating in the eucharist?

4. How are the three mysteries of the last supper, death, and resurrection related? Why are all three of them necessary?

5. How are we victims in the mass? How do we undergo the offering, death, and transformation in our own lives?

SIX

The Eucharist and the Other Sacraments

The other sacraments, as well as every ministry of the church, and every work of the apostolate, are linked with the holy eucharist and are directed toward it. For the most blessed eucharist contains the church's entire spiritual wealth, that is, Christ himself, our Passover and living bread. Through his very flesh, made vital and vitalizing by the Holy Spirit, he offers life to men. They are thereby invited and led to offer themselves, their labors, and all created things together with him. (*Decree on the Ministry and Life of Priests,* n. 5)

Over and over again the documents of Vatican II stress that the eucharist is the center of christian life. In the eucharist the multiplicity of persons, outlooks, and works achieve a unity. In the eucharist the christian's life reaches a fulfillment that leads into eternal life. The other sacramental acts of the church flow from the eucharist or set men in relation to it.

A central theme of the eucharist is fulfillment of the human person which takes place
through transformation. This transformation
involves the restructuring and re-orientation
of the whole personality. This is the central
sacramentalism of all the sacraments. This
pattern of transformation is established during the public life of Christ.

What actually took place at the marriage
feast in Cana, what St. John calls "the first
of Jesus' signs," was not the *creation* of wine.
The jars were not empty and suddenly filled
with wine. The servants filled the jars with
water, and then a miracle of transformation
took place. Water was changed to wine. Such
a transformation takes place in the sacraments
and achieves its perfection in the eucharist.

The significance of transformation, which
reaches its climax in the transubstantiation of
the gift of the christian community, is found
in the other sacraments. This points to the
whole mystery of grace. The life of grace and
the extension of grace in the transformation
of creation is not a creation from nothing. It
is the taking of something and making it
better, transforming it into something su-

perior. Just as the species of bread and wine are christianized, so through that instrumentality, the christian community is more deeply christianized. The notion of transformation is extremely important in approaching the relationship of the other sacraments to the eucharist.

Perhaps the best way to explain the relationship of the other sacraments to the eucharist is to explain how the christian sacraments came into being. Historically, the rituals used in the other sacraments did not begin with Christ. Their symbolism and ritual was a culmination of the centuries that preceded them. God's action in human history has constantly been one of transforming man, of transforming the whole meaning of human life. God's intervention in history has constantly been to transform the whole significance of man's history on earth. A close look at the Old Testament tells us that in those early centuries there was an introduction of new meaning into human insights. The insights were already present from natural religions and philosophies, but now they are placed in a different context. There is an injection of new meaning and emphasis into human institutions, into the symbolism which people were already using. Something new was introduced into the whole context of their human living.

Men have always tried to explain the order and the power which they observed in nature and which they observed in human society. These phenomena were explained in creative philosophical insights expressed through the imaginative perspective of myths. These myths had no reference to a precise historical event. They told a story which tried to explain how things got to be the way they were; how men were organized into society. Myths not only attempted to explain where things came from and the power of nature, but also tried to get the person to enter into them and control them. The ritual reflected this same aspect of the myths. The ritual was an attempt to establish a contact with whatever it was that was operative, so that the rite could control events. The ritual, like the myth, was an attempt to put meaning into reality and offer some explanation.

For the Old Testament, the meaning that is put into reality is the meaning of the one God, the transforming principle of significance in human life. The one God transforms every other insight and every other institution, because they are seen in the light of *this* God; he is the one who is operative. Therefore, in spite of all the superficial, surface resemblances of the Jewish law and social behavior to other ancient peoples, there is a fundamental difference. The difference is that their God is in their midst.

When the Son of God comes into the world through the incarnation, the institution of the christian sacrament takes place in a sense. Not in the technical sense, but God in becoming man takes on the full context of human experience and christianizes it.

In passing through birth, education, growth, experience, suffering, human communication, love, death and new life, he takes the whole course of our experience. He puts his meaning into human life, simply by undergoing it. Human life can never again be the same because the Son of God has died and passed into glorified life. Because of **this** there is a redeeming or christianizing of human life from within. All the significance of human life and human history are transformed by this personal element which is the meaning of Christ himself. Christ also picks especially significant contexts from our life which he sanctifies. These contexts will not merely change the intrinsic meaning of an experience like birth or eating or dying. They will also transform the cumulative historical significance which has been building—the whole historical meaning of Israel, Israel's life and Israel's growth, is now transformed.

Just as God's entrance into history in Old Testament times changed the meaning of human progress, so also Christ changed the dimensions of human life. Therefore the relationship of other sacraments in relation to the eucharist, or the institution of the sacraments, for that matter, is not a question of isolated moments which Christ set apart in a methodical way. In several cases, Christ took significant rites which were already in existence. For example, baptism was already a practice which had rich meaning; Christ added new meaning to it.

We cannot say that Christ instituted baptism at the time he was baptized by John, because christian baptism includes the significance of death and resurrection. Until Christ had died and risen there could not have been christian baptism. The christian sacraments are actions of Christ in the church and, therefore, there could be no christian baptism until he had sent his Holy Spirit into the church. The institution of the sacraments and their relationship to one another is an interwoven process, and many of the events of Christ's life are part of the insitution of sacraments.

The institution of the sacraments is varied. The institution of the eucharist, for example, involves the whole preparation of Christ's public life and the very special moment of the last supper. Even here the process is not completed. There must still be death and resurrection and the sending of the Spirit. There is a certain focus given at the last supper that would permit us to say that Christ instituted the sacrament then.

However, this is not so clear in some of the other sacraments. The sacrament of

matrimony is really a problem. In this sacrament Christ transforms the meaning of human marriage by identifying himself as the
bridegroom, and then gives himself to the
church in the eucharist. This is why the fifth
chapter of Ephesians, where it speaks of the
sacrament of matrimony (vv. 21-33), is
also the theology of grace. It is a passage
that gives a profound ecclesiology and a mag-
nificent theology of baptism and the eucharist. Baptism, matrimony and the eucharist
are one interwoven reality because Christ has
transformed the significant realities of human
life.

As far as marriage is concerned, we must
remember that St. Paul begins his epistle to
the Ephesians by speaking of the finality,
the fulfillment that is to come in Christ (Eph.
22-23). This is not to be understood chrono-
logically, but as a finality. All creation is interpreted by St. Paul in terms of the mystery
of Christ and his church, the mystery of
redemption, which means that nothing was
created apart from that finality which is
Christ. Marriage does not enter as something
new, but the relationship in marriage goes

into the revelation of Christ and takes on its
fullest meaning there.

Intrinsic to the experience of profound
human love necessary for unity and begetting
life, there is already a divine element, namely,
being itself is love which is life-giving. Therefore God brings the love and unity of marriage to a perfection and establishes it as the
sign, the sacrament, of God's love and unity.
Christ identified himself as the bridegroom
in the gospels. Thereby he does not add something superficially to marriage, but shows
forth the love of God for man which is expressed and imitated in christian marriage.
Christian marriage becomes the living out of
that total self-giving expressed in the eucharist; it is the living out of the passover
mystery.

In baptism, we enter into the mystery of
Christ, the mystery of his death and resurrection. We do not enter this mystery of Christ
fully, because this sacrament gives us the
breakthrough into the mystery of Christ and
the possibility of dialogue. We grow toward
a finality in Christ. A person is not a christian
because we have seen him baptized; rather he

is a christian because he is growing toward Christ.

There is an *ontological* reality that is achieved in baptism. There is a radical transformation that takes place even in an infant. Baptism gives the priesthood and gives grace. As the child moves into consciousness, there is the ever intensified indwelling of the Holy Spirit. As the child grows, the support of his christian family and environment is given him, a support which will lead him to a personal commitment to the mystery of Christ. This commitment is crystallized in confirmation.

All the elements which are found in confirmation are already present in baptism. Witness, mission, priesthood all apply to baptism. In confirmation there is nothing more than the deepening of christian consciousness. Because most christians are baptized in their childhood, they do not undergo the process of conversion. When we have reached conscious life we are confronted with the choice; we have to be converted to Christ and accept him and consciously enter into his mysteries. The process of conversion could culminate in confirmation as the intensification and the active involvement in christian life. Through the ritual of confirmation, a person fully declares himself for Christ and declares that he wills to live the paschal mystery.

Penance stands in relation to the eucharist because it is the reconciliation that takes place before the feast. Here we need only recall the prodigal son who is reconciled with his father and then the father gives a feast in honor of that reconciliation. Penance, like the other sacraments, is the sacrament of reconciliation for eucharistic union. Christ did not redeem us by the fact of his death on Calvary, but by his human acceptance of death. This acceptance of death is present in the eucharist. Therefore, penance is the sacrament that reconciles us to Christ's redemption. Once again we are able to be open to being redeemed. The sacramentality of this sacrament is precisely the fact of reconciliation with God.

The sacrament of the anointing of the sick must be understood in terms of the priestly function of Christ to which the christian was introduced at baptism. In accepting the priesthood, the christian has the responsibility of overcoming with Christ the various influences of evil in human life. In order to redeem, the christian himself must be free from evil. Sin, of course, is the most radical evil that keeps us from participating fully in redemption. But also, the christian must be free to some extent from physical evil. If I have a headache it is difficult to enter deeply into prayer. If I am dying of tuberculosis, it is difficult to retain christian hope, and difficult to enter into the total mystery of redemption. Consequently, a person needs redemption, not just from the central evil of sin, but also from conjoined physical evils insofar as they touch the human person.

In part, the sacrament exists to cure us of physical evil, but more importantly it exists to prevent physical evil from deeply touching the human person and keeping him from being a christian, from joining his suffering to those of Christ for the redemption of the world. The sacrament of the anointing of the sick is most important when the christian faces the hopeful human choice, when he has the great human experience of physically passing into the mystery of Christ through death, resurrection and final fulfillment.

The priesthood makes the mystery of the eucharist present so that the community of christians can share in the essential redemptive mysteries of Christ. He offers the total sacrifice of the christian community to the Father who transforms it into his Son and draws the community to that finality which is the fullness of Christ. The christian in his daily life extends the richness of Christ's humanity and mission to all history. The community brings the world community to the full meaning that Christ brought in his incarnation.

The full redemptive mystery celebrated in the eucharist is not, therefore, a mystery apart from the other sacraments, nor is it separate from the whole church. The sacraments are the actions of the church. The church could not exist without these redemptive acts which lead to her expression of unity in the eucharist. Without the sacraments, the church would be like a man without his essential faculties of intellect and will. This is why the church herself is called the sacrament of Christ. As a sacrament she expresses—the whole christian community expresses—the redemptive and transforming action of Christ. In a diversity of actions she exercises her sanctifying power, but always in relation to the mystery which she possesses in the eucharist.

The whole christian life is sacramental and expresses the presence of Christ. In the christian community, Christ is officially present and carries his redemptive work out through the seven official actions of redemption. The six sacraments stand in relation to the eucharist because they either reconcile us to the eucharist or help us to carry out the meaning of the eucharist in our daily lives, in the human community, in history, so that Christ may be first-born of all.

He is the image of the unseen God
    and the first-born of all creation,
    for in him were created
    all things in heaven and on earth:
    everything visible and invisible,

Thrones, Dominations, Sovereignties,
    Powers—
  all things were created through him and
    for him.
Before anything was created, he existed,
  and he holds all things in unity.
Now the church is his body,
  he is its head.
As he is the beginning,
  he was first to be born from the dead,
  so that he should be first in every way;
  because God wanted all perfection
  to be found in him
  and all things to be reconciled through
  him and for him,
  everything in heaven and everything on
    earth,
  when he made peace
  by his death on the cross.
                (Col. 1:15-20)

DISCUSSION QUESTIONS

1. Do you find the eucharist a unifying force in
   your life? Why or why not? Can the dif-

ficulties which arise in your discussion be overcome?

2. Why can the author say that the central theme of the eucharist is fulfillment of the human person?

3. How is each sacrament a moment of transformation in our life? How has Christ transformed the whole of human life?

4. Plan a eucharistic celebration which emphasizes the basic elements mentioned in this book.

Suggested Readings

Bernard Cooke, S.J. *Christian Sacraments and Christian Personality*. Chicago: Holt, Rinehart and Winston, 1965.

William F. Hogan. *Christ's Redemptive Sacrifice*. Englewood Cliffs, N.J.: Prentice-Hall, 1963.

John H. Miller. *Signs of Transformation in Christ*. Englewood Cliffs, N.J.: Prentice-Hall, 1963.

John P. Schanz. *The Sacraments of Life and Worship*. Milwaukee: Bruce, 1966.

Edward Schillebeeckx, O.P. *Christ the Sacrament of the Encounter with God*. New York: Sheed and Ward, 1963.

_____. *The Eucharist*. New York: Sheed and Ward, 1968.

Multi-Media

An American Mass Program. This record presents hymns for congregational singing in the tradition of the Negro spiritual. The simplicity and the spontaneity of the music allow it to be mastered rapidly. This music is helpful in developing a more popular attitude toward the mass. *33⅓, 12″ record, monaural only. Composer and artist: Clarence Rivers. Produced by the Queen's Men Drama Guild. Distributed by the World Library of Sacred Music. Sale $4.79.*

Cup and Covenant. This filmstrip attempts to help the viewer develop a better understanding of the social implications of the sacrament of the lord's supper. The presentation is biblically oriented; the eucharist is seen as the sign of our union with Christ. *63-frame filmstrip, color, guide, record with automatic inaudible and non-automatic audible signals. Thomas S. Klise Co., P.O. Box 3418, Peoria, Illinois 61414. Sold by producer: $16:50. For rent from some religious filmstrip libraries.*

In the Name of Jesus Christ, Let's Celebrate.
This series of filmstrips is designed to help the
viewer broaden and deepen his perspective on
what it means to celebrate the liturgy. Liturgy
in these frames refers to baptism, the eucharist
and the five minor sacraments. This series
brings together daily experience and man's
celebration of them through an inter-relation
of the sacraments. *Six 49-59 frame filmstrips,
color, guide, six records with automatic inaudible and non automatic audible signals.
Produced by the Liturgical Conference, 1968.
Sold by Thomas S. Klise Co. (see above):
$89.50 per set. For rent from some religious
filmstrip libraries.*

The Mass. The main thrust of these photos of the
different parts of the mass is to orient the
student to the proper roles of the people and
the celebrant. A guide, "God's Family at
Worship," by J. Richard Quinn, a thematic
index, and separate caption cards are included
in the set. *One set of fourteen posters, 17" x
22", black and white. Published by Geo. A.
Pflaum, 38 West 5th Street, Dayton, Ohio
45402. Available from publisher and many
bookstores: $6.00 per set.*

The Supper. This film touches people directly
and delivers joy. It is about the attempt of
one person to make contact with another.

What happens is a combination of suspense and surprise. It is very helpful in understanding the eucharist as an every day event and a ritual that can be carried out in daily living. *Augsburg Publishing House, 426 South 5th Street, Minneapolis, Minnesota 55415. 55 minutes. Black and White. Rent: $20.00.*

Understanding the Liturgy. This series of filmstrips (3 sets, 2 parts) is very helpful in understanding the meaning of the liturgy. Sets 1 and 2 are exceptionally well illustrated by contemporary artist Frank Hopper. Set 3 features color photography of various parts of the mass with black and white inserts of contemporary secular actions and events. The first two sets are highly recommended to explain the ritual expression of the exodus and Christ's passover in our eucharistic celebration. *3 sets of filmstrips (2 filmstrips each), aproximately 30 minutes per set, color, guides, records with either automatic inaudible signal or non-automatic audible signal. Produced by Alpha Corporation of America. Distributed by John P. Daleiden Co., 1530 N. Sedgwick Street, Chicago, Ill. 60610: $31.95 per set, $95.85 per series.*